TRIUMPH IN THE MIDST OF TRAGEDY
SURVIVING A CATEGORY 5 HURRICANE

ETHLENE MCINTOSH

© 2020 Divine Works Publishing LLC.

TRIUMPH IN THE MIDST OF TRAGEDY: SURVIVING A CATEGORY 5 HURRICANE

ALL RIGHTS RESERVED. No part of this publication may be reproduced, stored in a retrieval system, or transmitted in any form or by any means, electronic, mechanical, photocopying, recording or otherwise without the prior permission of the publisher or in accordance with the provisions of the Copyright, Designs, and Patents Act 1988 or under the terms of any license permitting limited copying issued by the Copyright Licensing Agency.

The views expressed in this work are solely those of the author and do not necessarily reflect the views of the publisher, the publisher hereby disclaims any responsibility for them.

Printed in the United States of America
First Edition: 2020

Scripture taken from the King James Version®., (unless otherwise noted), Copyright © 1982 by Thomas Nelson. Used by permission. All rights reserved.

ISBN 13: 978-1-949105-99-5 (Paperback)
ISBN 13: 978-1-949105-33-9 (eBook)

Published by:
Divine Works Publishing, LLC
Royal Palm Beach, Florida USA

www.DivineWorksPublishing.com
561-990-BOOK (2665)

DEDICATION

This book is dedicated to the memory of my late mother, Evelyn Algertha McIntosh Nee Poitier; a precious gem. She was my mentor and confidant; a woman of strong faith and excellent character who taught me how to pray and trust God in every situation. She was a prayer warrior and a wonderful example of the Proverbs 31 woman.
I will forever cherish her memory.

TABLE OF CONTENTS

FOREWORD | *ix*
INTRODUCTION | *xi*

CHAPTER ONE
 My Past Experience | 1

CHAPTER TWO
 The Hurricane of the Century: A Horrific Experience | 5

CHAPTER THREE
 D-Day (Mounting Fear and Desperation) | 7

CHAPTER FOUR
 The Misleading Mythical Eye | 11

CHAPTER FIVE
 An Onslaught from the Opposite Direction | 13

CHAPTER SIX
 Venturing Outside | 15

CHAPTER SEVEN
 Our Search for Missing Family Members | 17

CHAPTER EIGHT
 The Return Home | 21

CHAPTER NINE
 Leaving the Island | 25

CHAPTER TEN
 A Joyful Reunion | 29

CHAPTER ELEVEN
 Finding Assistance | 33

CHAPTER TWELVE
 Tragedy and Triumph | 37

CHAPTER THIRTEEN
 Our Gratitude | 41

CHAPTER FOURTEEN
 Lessons from Dorian | 43

FOREWORD

Ms. Ethlene McIntosh is the second daughter of Rev. Ezekiel McIntosh and the Late Evelyn McIntosh of Wood Cay, North Abaco, The Bahamas. Ethlene spent her formative years in the tranquil settlement of Wood Cay where she became entrenched in the traditional way of life germane to the ethos of the era.

Ethlene attended the Fox Town All-age School and later relocated to New Providence where she completed her high school education at C. C. Sweeting High School.

Hewn out of the 'rock' of philanthropy and scholarship, coupled with the assurance of the Call of God on her life, Ethlene, matriculated to College of the Bahamas where she fulfilled the requirements for her certification as a Trained Teacher with her Major being Social Science and Language Arts.

Given Ethlene's insatiable appetite for advanced training as it relates to the Pedagogy of Teaching, coupled with the Management Systems related thereto, she further engaged in advanced studies culminating in the attainment of a Bachelor of Arts Degree in Education and a Masters (of Arts) Degree in Business Administration.

Pursuant to the above, Ethlene availed herself of numerous travel opportunities which further enhanced her appreciation for and knowledge of the diverse people and cultures of the world. The latter, no doubt, served her well infusing a greater level of dynamism at both the classroom and management levels as it related to the domains of Social Science and Language Arts.

This masterpiece, Triumph in The Midst of Tragedy, is yet another series of vignettes released by this gifted author which, no doubt, will serve as an educational tool for both present and future generations as the phenomenon of Climate Change manifests itself in increasingly more violent hurricanes and other weather systems.

That this educative Work of Art should serve as a tool of enlightenment for many across our geographical region and beyond for both old and young, I have no doubt!
Congratulations and Best Wishes!

Dr. Lenora J. Black (Ph.D)

INTRODUCTION

The events of September 1, 2019, will forever remain embedded within the deepest crevices of my mind. Ferocious, unrelenting winds, ongoing rains—like a rushing river, and the sound of debris smashing violently against our house etched lasting memories of the ravages of hurricanes. It was on this date that hurricane Dorian slammed into our island as a category 5 hurricane, with record breaking wind speed, and storm surges of more than twenty feet. The Bahamas is an archipelago made up of more than 700 islands, rocks, and cays. Hurricane Dorian tracked across the Atlantic in what appeared to be a direct path toward the Bahamas. It seemed as if something hideous and evil, monster-like, was hell-bent on devouring its prey.

As early as August 26th, the National Hurricane Center warned of the potential threat of tropical storm Dorian and the possibility of it affecting the Bahamas. Later that week on August 30th, the government of the Bahamas issued a hurricane warning for the northwestern Bahamas. These islands include the Abacos, Berry Islands, Bimini, Eleuthera, Grand Bahama Island, Andros and New Providence. Hurricane shelters were identified and persons in low lying areas were encouraged to evacuate. Shortly thereafter, it was revealed that Abaco and Grand Bahama would suffer a direct hit if the hurricane remained on its projected path. A compelling, clarion call for immediate evacuation was heralded throughout the would-be affected islands.

On September 1st, 2019 Hurricane Dorian made landfall in Abaco as a category five hurricane. One day later it hit Grand Bahama in the same category, exiting on September 3rd.

Hurricane Dorian is recorded as the most intense tropical cyclone on record to strike the Bahamas and is regarded as the worst natural disaster in the country's history. Indeed, the effects of Hurricane Dorian in the Bahamas were far reaching. It was anticipated that the death toll would be staggering and reports estimated damage of more than three billion dollars. There were at least 70 deaths in the country and more than 280 persons were left missing.

CHAPTER ONE

MY PAST EXPERIENCE

From an early age I knew about hurricanes. They came around almost annually during the months of August and September. As a child, I looked forward to the excitement of hurricanes. It was the sound of howling winds and heavy rains beating against the doors and windows that was exhilarating. We would be locked in for a day or two until the hurricane passed. We'd wait impatiently for my grandfather to open the door so we could see what outside looked like; oranges, grapefruit, bananas, limes and avocados, not to mention sugar apples and hog plums; could be seen scattered on the ground amidst fallen trees. My grandfather would be near to tears as a result of the loss, while the kids screamed, jumped and ran around gleefully exploring the whole settlement.

For my siblings and me, it was a fun time. During one of the hurricanes, the water around the yard was so high that we paddled in wash tubs collecting what was left of the fruits. It was exciting!

TRIUMPH IN THE MIDST OF TRAGEDY

My grandfather never failed to warn us that hurricanes could be dangerous. He recounted numerous hurricanes of the past that were devastating. My mother also shared how she lost several close family members during a dangerous hurricane. For example, she recounted how one of her aunts and several offspring were traveling by boat unaware of a lurking hurricane as there were no radios available to provide a forecast. Unfortunately, the hurricane was upon them before they could get to land resulting in the death of my mother's aunt and several of her children.

My father also related his experience of a dangerous hurricane in 1949. He along with his father, grandfather and two uncles left Pine Ridge, Grand Bahama for Abaco. They were traveling by sail boat and since the weather was very calm the boat moved at snail pace. Although they had heard that a hurricane was traveling before setting sail from Grand Bahama, they had no means of receiving accurate information concerning the hurricane. Suddenly, without warning, as they neared Mangrove Cay not far from Pine Ridge the winds became so fierce that they had to quickly remove the sail and cut the mast to prevent the boat from capsizing. At this point, the ropes to which both anchors were attached broke. Realizing that they were in grave danger, they tied the dinghy boat on to the deck of the big boat but at the same time a huge wave hit the boat knocking the dinghy from one side to the other and then overboard taking his grandfather with it. Since it was extremely dark by this time no one saw that his grandfather had been thrown overboard with the dinghy. They were all shocked and surprised a few minutes later to see his grandfather climbing into the boat. His grandfather explained that after he hit the water, he grabbed onto a piece of rope that was still holding the dinghy to the big boat. He struggled against the waves and was finally able to pull himself

MY PAST EXPERIENCE

back into the boat. Later the small boat broke away and was lost. From all indications, it appeared as though the big boat would be destroyed as it continued furiously rocking from side to side and drifting at a rapid pace.

As a last resort, amidst much prayer they took the balance (pig iron) that was used for balancing the boat and fastened them to the ropes that held the anchors earlier. This slowed the pace at which the boat was drifting. After several hours, the winds subsided and the following morning they found themselves near a little Cay off Abaco called Sails Cay. Here they were able to repair the mast and hoist the sail again enabling them to arrive at their destination on the mainland of Abaco.

In the early years, there was little to no newscast available to most people, particularly those living in the Family Islands. As a result, many could not follow the path of hurricanes or detect the eye of the hurricane. What is interesting to note however, was that most of the older people knew when bad weather was coming by simply observing the sky and the sea.

They also knew how to prepare and protect their families during hurricanes. Low thatched huts were constructed in many communities to be used as hurricane shelters. On some islands, inhabitants took refuge in caves until the weather had passed.

As I grew older, I came to realize that hurricanes are dangerous, tumultuous, unavoidable, natural occurrences that wreaked havoc by destroying homes, businesses, lives, and often people's future.

I vividly recall the ravages of hurricane Floyd in September of 1999 when I returned to Abaco to find my family overwhelmed without any drinking water and very little food left. The interior of their house was badly damaged as salt water had risen some eighteen inches in their home. Additionally, tons of debris covered the yard where they lived. My father, a farmer, endured great losses as his farm, along with his disc machine were destroyed, not to mention the numerous fruit trees around the house. His fish house, electric corn mill, appliances and furniture were also badly damaged. Further, my father's walk-in freezer had been swept yards away from the house and destroyed. The freezer, a key part of his livelihood, was where he kept the crawfish he purchased from the men in the community to be later resold. Everything was lost. His business was ruined. Adding to this devastation, was the loss of electrical power and running water. I began quickly cleaning up the debris. It took days to complete this arduous chore. The devastation was overwhelming.

It took about two years before there were any visible signs of rebuilding and recovery. Sadly, this was short-lived. Five years after hurricane Floyd, came hurricane Frances in 2004, closely followed by hurricane Jeanne. Both hurricanes ripped through Abaco destroying vegetation, tearing off roofs, and dumping several inches of water on parts of the island. Again my family's homestead was compromised. This time, I went home to find many discouraged and disillusioned Islanders. My parents were among them; they had lost a part of their roof and had experienced much water damage. "We ain't back on our feet good yet and hurricane again" was the common cry throughout the community. "Anyhow, thank God for life, we just have to start over again." Once again recovery efforts began as many houses had to be rebuilt or repaired.

These experiences caused me to take hurricanes seriously. Every year just before hurricane season, I would begin to pray for protection over our islands.

In 2016, we were threatened by hurricane Matthew. My family and I prayed and the storm turned resulting in minimal damage.

CHAPTER TWO

THE HURRICANE OF THE CENTURY: A HORRIFIC EXPERIENCE

In late August of 2019, we learned of an approaching hurricane named Dorian. The community went about as usual without much concern. As I mentioned earlier, hurricanes are common occurrences in our country. Many hoped that it would go away, as they sometimes do. If it would not turn away from us then we expected little damage from it. However, the intensity and speed of this hurricane became of major concern to us by August 30th as hurricane Dorian refused to die. Instead it lifted its ugly head and steered its course straight towards us. Tensions began to grow, schools closed, and residents rushed to the grocery stores in large numbers in anticipation of the onslaught—not knowing what to expect, but preparing for the worse. By Saturday August 31st, it was difficult to find parking or get into any the food stores.

As I sat at home later that day and listened to the forecast, I realized that this storm was unlike any other we had experienced. It's wind speed continued rapidly increasing. I began to pray for mercy. It was nearing category five. I felt what seemed to be a heavy sense of depression and tears began to weld up in my eyes. Why was I feeling such heaviness in my spirit? I continued to pray as I prepared the rolls and seasoned meat in preparation for the hurricane. I contacted family member's abroad and requested prayers, because I knew that the communication system would soon shut down if the wind speeds continued on. As if glued to the television set, I listened intently to the weather report which continued to indicate that the hurricane would hit Abaco by Sunday afternoon, September 1st. The speed and intensity of this approaching hurricane brought much concern. I continued to pray for protection.

Close family members began to gather at our home, which is customary for us during hurricanes. We usually try to ride out storms together. At about 9:00 pm on Saturday night as I prayed, I heard the Holy Spirit saying "go to the marina, stretch your hands toward the water and command it not to come". Taking one of my sisters with me, I walked toward the marina. The fierce winds were already against us. We fought against the wind to get as near to the marina as possible and then followed the instruction.

Upon returning to the house, everyone went to bed, but I continued to pray until late into the night. There was grave concern for our lives. This impending hurricane stirred within me an uncertainty that is still hard to describe, yet at the same time it ignited a measure of faith that was parellel to that fear. Amidst the dread, I remained prayerful.

CHAPTER THREE

D-DAY
(MOUNTING FEAR & DESPERATION)

At about 6:00 am, on Sunday September 1st, I walked toward the kitchen to begin preparing breakfast. I approached the window to see what the weather looked like outside. To my amazement, my gaze fell upon a huge angel standing with his hands stretched out toward the house. I jolted back in fear. I then heard the voice of the Lord saying, *"your house will not fall, you have been praying for weeks, your house will not fall"*. It took me a few minutes to compose myself and then I shared with my sister what I had seen and what the Lord had spoken.

We continued the breakfast preparation and fed those who were in the house. There were about twelve persons in total. These were family members and friends who had come to ride out the hurricane with us. Included in this number were five children ranging in ages from 4-10 years and my father who was nearing the age of eighty five.

The winds were becoming fierce. Our major concern was for one of my brothers, who should have joined us by then, but had not yet arrived. He lived some sixty miles away and was on his way. When we finally got in contact with him, he indicated that the winds were already strong, debris had fallen into the road, and as such, he had to drive slowly. By 10:00 am he telephoned to say that he could not make it to our house because the water from the sea, in the area where we lived, had already covered the streets and it had become too dangerous to continue. We encouraged him to turn around and get to a shelter quickly.

Fortunately, he was able to drive to another sister who lived in a nearby settlement. Less than an hour later, the ceiling fans on the back porch of our house began to fly away one by one. The noise of debris could be heard slamming against the windows, doors and railings. There was much concern. This storm was scheduled to hit us between one and two o'clock, but by 11:00 am it appeared that it was upon us.

By 1:00pm this monster hurricane slammed in at full force. We later learned that wind speed was up to 185 miles per hour with gusts of 225 miles per hour. Houses rocked and reeled from side to side. Accompanying the high winds were raging sea surges—more than twenty feet high in some areas. Few could withstand this raging storm. Within minutes houses were ripped from their foundations or collapsed as the waters rushed through leaving behind only rubble. Buildings built to the country's code standard gave way to the wrath of Dorian.

The ferocious winds threatened our safety. It seemed as if our house would blow away at any moment. Heavy rains beat against the house finally lashing its way through the sides of the double glass door at the back of the house. The door shook fiercely; we ran for the mops, brooms and buckets in an attempt to keep the water out. We also grabbed towels and blankets to soak up the water, but to no avail. We finally decided to leave it alone.

D-DAY (MOUNTING FEAR & DESPERATION)

Our major concern now was whether or not the door would be compromised. The windows and door were hurricane proof and had not been covered. It was obviously too late to think of putting up shutters though several sheets of plywsood were stored in the garage. An urgent meeting was called to provide instructions on what to do if the house became compromised. However, I remained resolute in my faith in God and quickly reminded everyone that the house would not fall. God had spoken! Had I not heard and believed God, I would have panicked. It seemed impossible for our house to survive this ferocious 'demon.' It reminded me of the scripture in John 10:10, which reads, *"The thief (Satan) comes only to kill, steal and destroy..."*

Windows, doors, the roof and indeed the entire house was being pounded on by flying debris. Our house was taking a beating, but God said it would not fall. I could still see the image of the huge angel with hands stretched toward the house. I knew we would be safe. My mind quickly flashed back to *Psalm 91:1-4 "He that dwelleth in the secret place of the Most High, shall abide under the shadow of the Almighty. I will say of the Lord, he is my refuge and my fortress: my God; in Him will I trust. Surely He will deliver thee from the snare of the fowler and from the noisome pestilence. He shall cover thee with his feathers and under his wings shall thou trust"*

For nearly two hours our house was bombarded non—stop as we waited out this first part of the hurricane. It sounded like a war zone with heavy tanks just rolling through the land. This hurricane unleashed its fury with all its arsenals and declared outright war on us. It seemed like a marathon. When would it end? There was nothing we could do, but wait and trust God's mercy.

CHAPTER FOUR

THE MISLEADING MYTHICAL EYE

I had been told that the second part of a hurricane was usually more severe than the first. The eye of the hurricane finally came and all was calm, but we knew that this would be short-lived. We hurried outside to see what had happened. I was awestruck. Many roofs or parts of roofs were gone in our community and the windows and doors of most homes were blown out. Added to this were fallen houses and piles of debris. Trees were tossed everywhere, many were pulled up from the roots. I thought to myself if this was not the worst of the hurricane, then what would happen after the eye passed.

Most of the trees in our yard were gone. The once stately palm trees that adorned the front of our yard were thrown across or resting alongside the remains of huge Gumelemi and Madeira trees yards away. Avocados were strewn all over the ground. This was the first bearing from one of our two trees and oh how we looked forward to eating those avocados. Our sugar apple trees, our Jujube (Juju) tree with fruits almost full, our papaya and soursop trees were all uprooted and shredded. Wow! We were lost for words. To my utter dismay, my huge rosemary plant was destroyed. I had spent so much time nurturing this precious plant. Its aroma added much flavor to most of my dishes. Shock, amazement and a heavy heart overwhelmed me. The only word that escaped my lips was "Wow!!" I began to choke as I forced back the tears.

Painfully aware that we had only a short window before the second part of the hurricane was upon us, I turned to go back inside. Suddenly, I heard a cry for help coming from one of our neighbors. Other family members heard it and turned toward the house. We saw a frantic elderly lady attempting to climb over the railing with a suitcase. Several of us ran to assist her. Their house had been compromised and there was a panic to get out. The others followed and we took them to our house to wait out the second part of the storm.

After assisting our neighbors, we quickly closed up the house and braced ourselves for what would come next.

CHAPTER FIVE

AN ONSLAUGHT FROM THE OPPOSITE DIRECTION

The raging storm continued with heavy winds and rain but with less debris hitting the house. Those rescued huddled near one of the closets while family members sat around the kitchen counter or sprawled out on chairs in the sitting room. The manhole cover began rising and falling; every time it did there was a huge puff of wind blowing in the surrounding area. At times it felt as if the roof would lift. Suddenly, a loud cracking sound came from one of the bathrooms. Two of the children who were near that area ran in a panic to the kitchen shouting: "the bathroom window blew out". We ran to check and sure enough it was gone. Concerns mounted: what would it look like when this is over? Did all of our people survive? What would Abaco be like after this? Would we have to leave? Tears filled our eyes as we posed these questions.

After more than two hours of pounding rain and ferocious winds, the weather began to settle slowly. Supper was prepared and everyone fed. There was little conversation now as most of us were tired, weary, and much relieved from the day's proceedings. We began setting up blow up beds wherever we could find a dry spot. All remaining blankets, sheets, and towels from the linen closet were utilized to ensure the comfort of all.

After everyone was settled in bed, I stayed awake most of the night and prayed as we waited.

CHAPTER SIX

VENTURING OUTSIDE

Strong winds and rain lasted into the morning hours of Monday. At crack of dawn, we tried to venture outdoors to see the additional damage and to check the neighborhood, but to no avail. The strong winds and rain beat heavily against our faces with a stinging and painful effect that forced us to retreat into our dwelling.

It was not until later on in the day that we left our house amidst the rain and wind to find a path to the main road. We pushed our way through large puddles of dirty water, fallen houses, broken fences, and massive heaps of debris. We maneuvered through a business house, though still standing, the interior had been completely washed out by the storm surge. We finally made it to the main road. The sight was indescribable. Places where colorful waterfront restaurants and marinas stood just hours before had been reduced to mere rubble. Was this reality or a dream? I tried to think of words to describe the scene—catastrophic, horrific, devastation, disaster, mass destruction. Was this judgement day? What were we to make of this? Should we laugh, cry, or wait to awake from this nightmare?

The massive piles of debris blocked the street preventing us from going to the west and so we went east. A sense of horror filled the air. It appeared as if most of the electrical poles had been uprooted and dumped in all directions with no concern for property— they were sprawled on top of vehicles, buildings and boats that seemed to have been airlifted to land. Surrounding trees were so hard hit that they were without leaves and appeared parched and dry. As we walked, I questioned if this was real. Am I seeing correctly? Nothing seemed to have escaped the wrath of Dorian.

There were a few people on the street. Some were walking aimlessly as if in a drunken stupor. We asked if they were OK. The horror stories unfolded. They were homeless trying to make sense of this dilemma. One gentleman with a towel wrapped around his body and one foot of slippers told us that the fierce winds and water rushed through his house taking him at an estimated fifty miles per hour through the streets of Marsh Harbour. He finally caught onto a tree and was able to survive until the winds subsided. Another individual pointed to his house in the distance that had been gutted out by powerful waves. Furniture from his house was cited more than half a mile away while his vehicles were totally destroyed.

We walked for more than a mile past guest houses, hotels, and other business places that had been utterly destroyed or severely damaged. Bicycles, boats of all shapes and sizes, furniture of all types, along with scores of vehicles were strewn everywhere in sight. After speaking with those we met along the way we returned home saddened and filled with grave concerns.

CHAPTER SEVEN

OUR SEARCH FOR MISSING FAMILY MEMBERS

What was most frightening was that we could not hear from other family members who lived on the island—even those who lived in close proximity to us. Later that morning, we forced our way like brave soldiers, crawling through fallen buildings, seeking a path to find other relatives. From the look of things, it seemed that few would have survived this tragedy. We pushed our way, for what seemed hours, through dirty water up to our knees. Every commercial bank on the island had been decimated. Off a distance, a man made his way from one of the banks with what appeared to be a large bag of coins. Liberal amounts of wood from one hardware store scattered in all directions. Gas stations were quiet, most with little structures remaining. It was difficult to recognize where we were at times because the scenery had changed significantly.

As we neared the port (docking facility), it was clear that the two largest shanty towns on the island occupied mainly by migrants had collapsed. The Mudd and the Pigeon Pea were in shambles. These communities had existed for decades near the waterfront facing the port. Needless to say they had grown tremendously occupying quite a large area of land. Fallen roofs, buildings, pieces of clothing, and other household items could be seen at a distance. The smell of death lingered in the air. Water and fallen debris made it difficult to continue on our projected path and so we turned around in search of another path that was less difficult to maneuver.

Strong winds continued, as what appeared to be looters pushed their way into stores and pillaged whatever Dorian had not taken. Many with trolleys, others with large black garbage bags, buckets, pans, clothes baskets, rugs, pots, paint, various types of appliances, were all being packed and carried away. Children could be seen with parents trying on shoes in the shoe store, ravaging through goods in other stores—children carried containers with stockings, socks, and other items of clothing.

Further down many walked with cases of water, juice, chips, and other items from a local warehouse. I thought perhaps my eyes were failing me. We continued our journey searching for my family. Finally, we arrived at the Government Complex which housed the Command Centre. Surely, we would get some answers here. However, it was not what we had expected. The area was crowded with hundreds of people who had to flee the shelters and were now homeless. Pungent smells of human waste filled the air. We pushed our way through searching for persons in authority, but to no avail. We looked around for security officers, but there was none visible. Finally we saw a lady, who we recognized, who seemed distraught. She told us that she had lost everything and was herself in search of missing relatives.

We then moved to the Department of Education housed in this complex. Here we were greeted by what appeared to be migrants, who now occupied cubicles and offices that belonged to education officers and other workers from The Ministry of Education. They were unable to provide any assistance.

Our next decision was to walk to the nearby Government Clinic. As we were about to exit the Government Complex we approached a familiar face. This gentleman indicated that he had seen my brother somewhere since the hurricane, but could not provide us an exact location. However, this was welcomed news that brought us hope as we continued.

On arrival at the Clinic, hundreds of individuals were outside milling around. The nearby street and the lawn at the clinic were lined with damaged vehicles.

An American helicopter had just landed on the grounds of the clinic. We knew without asking that they were bringing in the injured or dead. Our entrance into the clinic revealed a most unbelievable sight. Hundreds of individuals were standing, sitting, and lying along the corridors. As we pushed our way through this sea of human faces, we inquired of those we knew if any of our relatives had been seen, but again there were no positive response. We canvassed the area for a while holding on to each other, peeping into rooms, and listening to horror stories. Persons claimed that there were many injured and that they had witnessed a disturbingly large number of dead bodies brought in. This news brought much heaviness to our hearts and finally we exited to make the long journey to where my sister and her family lived.

The pelting rain and dangerous winds continued. We covered our faces with jackets and scarfs to prevent the pain of the impact of this unwelcomed weather. It was extremely difficult, but we were undeterred as we were prepared to not stop until we brought closure to the matter. As such, we trudged on with wet blistered toes and heels in the hope of accomplishing our mission. After some forty five minutes we neared the area where my sister and her family lived. In the distance we could see what appeared to be a sea. The streets were impassable leading to further disappointment, fear, and frustration. Our concern became greater. Did they survive this escapade? Would we see them alive again? I prayed and felt a peace in my spirit.

We tried to take another path but met even larger puddles of water. However, we could now view the houses in the area. It was clear that their roof had been compromised and roofs beyond their house had been blown off. We continued inquiring in the community but again no one had seen or heard from them.

Eventually, after exhausting all avenues we made our way back home.

CHAPTER EIGHT

THE RETURN HOME

There were far more people on the streets now. A number of vehicles, many with broken or no windows, obviously damaged by the hurricane, were crawling through the deep water along the main street of Marsh Harbor piled with goods from various stores. Again, the number of pedestrians increased significantly, as more goods were being carried in the direction of the Government Complex and the Clinic.

We waded through the water again and decided to change course in order to escape walking through so much dirty water a second time. Soon we discovered that this was not a good decision as many buildings had fallen into the streets and there was water everywhere. Exhausted and overwhelmed, we finally made it back home.

Two of my sisters decided that they would take the Kayak the following day and paddle through the water to get to the home of our other family members. Fear of the unknown began to set in as the evening passed. One sister broke into a loud outburst of crying; "What if they are not alive", she mourned. "If they were alright, I know they would have made an effort to get to us." We tried to console her. Her comment brought tears to all of our eyes.

We waited through the long night in anticipation of daybreak. Two of my siblings along with a niece and a friend who were at the house gathered the kayaks, paddles, and pumps to make the journey of exploration. I stayed home, because I felt that all was well, and believed that the family members we were concerned for were waiting for the water to subside to come to us. By this time, American helicopters on rescue missions could be seen everywhere providing assistance.

After their departure, I busied myself cleaning the house, and hanging out the wet towels, sheets and rugs. Around ten o'clock my sibling who stayed with me accompanied me to help put out the garbage. As we were doing so, she screamed and began running toward the gate. My eyes suddenly caught the excitement; my brother, my sister, and my brother-in-law whom we had earlier searched for were now walking toward us. I dropped the bags of garbage, screamed with joy, and ran with open arms to greet them. Though they were exhausted, wet, and dirty, we embraced them with much fervor. It was a welcome sight.

Once back inside the house, we provided them with a hot meal as they shared about their experience. During the hurricane their house roof had been badly compromised. Adding to this, they discovered that the water outside was up to the window ledge and rising. As such, they took shelter in an apartment building at the back of their house, but later the water found its way inside. In trying to escape to another building nearby, they discovered that the roof had completely blown off.

For three days they stayed in a vehicle swimming to and

from the house to retrieve canned goods in order to eat. The water level was too high for them to get to the main road or surrounding buildings that were still standing. They eventually found a path through bushes and made it to the front street. Through water, debris, devastation, disaster and even floating bodies, they made their way to where we lived. The story was heart wrenching, but seeing them alive overshadowed all of that. Just to embrace them again meant everything to us.

Later we learned that my siblings who had gone in search of my relatives made it to the house and spoke with others who were there in the area. They soon arrived back home, having already heard the news that all our other family members were safe. After a wonderful time of embracing each other and thanking God for his protection, we walked them to the main road through a path that we had found with much debris but little water. We said our goodbyes as they left to return to their home with the promise to return the following morning to bathe and get a hot breakfast.

CHAPTER NINE

LEAVING THE ISLAND

As we began to move around the community there were many horror stories of missing persons and of bodies trapped under rubble. Foreign and local news media were everywhere capturing details of this catastrophic event. Many exclaimed that they had never witnessed this degree of destruction anywhere in the world. Soon there was concern of an epidemic. Authorities suggested we leave the island as quickly as possible. We knew that this would be difficult for us, because the only street that would take us to the main road was blocked with piles of debris which made it impassable. Tractors were clearing the main road, but were not authorized to clean side streets according to the drivers. With cutlass, pick-axes and saws, my family members took to the street and began the arduous task of clearing a path big enough for vehicles to drive through. This took several hours and intense labor, but the mission was accomplished by late evening.

Later we received word that airplanes would be available to take persons to New Providence the following day. We rapidly packed our belongings and made it to the airport by 11:00 am the next morning. Thousands were already gathered awaiting instruction from those who were in charge. After a brief wait, my family was allowed inside, through security and into the waiting area. We waited for some five hours without any information. As we were contemplating what to do next, we saw two relatives from Nassau walking toward us. They had earlier arrived at the Treasure Cay airport by charter, but were unable to reach us since all communication systems were down. As such, they hiked a ride to the Marsh Harbour Airport in hopes of finding us. After many embraces and much gratitude, they informed us that they were trying to charter two five seater planes to take us to Nassau, but could not guarantee that permission would be granted for them to fly into Abaco.

We quickly hired a taxi and made our way to Treasure Cay Airport. The ride was most frightening as the taxi driver had to maneuver around numerous fallen electrical lines as well as various types of debris, often pressing the gas pedal abruptly. It took us just over an hour and a half to arrive at the airport.

Hundreds of people were gathered—some milling around, others standing still with looks of grave concern on their faces and yet others sharing the horror stories of Dorian. Many had only the clothes left on their backs.

I scanned the crowd as I walked toward the area. Everyone-- rich, poor, white, black, young and old seemed to have been reduced to the same level. Dorian showed no favoritism, made no distinction, and certainly was no respecter of persons.

My attention then turned to a Bahamasair plane parked at the airport. As an agent walked past us, we inquired as to the procedure for traveling on the plane and were informed that we only needed to pay $75.00 (seventy--five dollars) per person and that would guarantee us a seat. We waited in anticipation that our planes would be allowed to make the trip. Fortunately, in less than an hour of waiting the planes landed and most of my family members were able to get out of Abaco that afternoon.

CHAPTER TEN

A JOYFUL REUNION

As we entered the terminal building in New Providence, scores of relatives who lived in the area of New Providence gathered and were overjoyed to see us. They had already placed us on the missing persons list as they were unable to make contact with us since the hurricane. We were taken to the home of one of my sisters where a scrumptious meal had been prepared. They were so thankful that we were alive and listened intently as we rehearsed every detail of the horrors of Dorian.

After several hours, they took us to the various living accommodations that had been prepared for us. We were always a close knit family, but hurricane Dorian created a closer bonding than before.

With heart-felt thanks and appreciation, I humbly expressed my indebtedness to my siblings and other relatives in New Providence for the great support and the major role they played in providing transportation, food, clothing, and finances during this disaster. Indeed, they all ensured that we were comfortable and graced us with their presence and a listening ear regularly. Words cannot express my gratitude. To God be the Glory!!

Over the next few days, I was amazed at the number of phone calls from friends, some of whom I had not seen or heard from in months. The warm gestures, offer of assistance, prayers and words of encouragement was overwhelming. It was during this ordeal that I came to appreciate even more, the value of true friends and how much they cared.

News out of Abaco soon revealed that the Bahamas government, along with other groups and organizations were providing free air services for victims of hurricane Dorian. Boats were also dispatched to the island bringing hundreds of persons at a time to New Providence. Within days almost an entire community was evacuated to New Providence. Some were placed in shelters provided by government and private organizations while others went to live with relatives or found rental accommodations.

Many of the older residents who survived this hurricane recalled that this was the second major evacuation for Abaco due to hurricanes. After the 1935 hurricane, the areas of Cornish Town and Ole Place located just east of Fire Road were so badly devastated that the government relocated residents between 1939 and 1941 to the present day Dundas Town and Murphy Town. My father's grandfather (on his mother's side) was a resident of Cornish Town at the time. Each family was allotted five acres of land for a small fee of five pounds. Small wooden houses 10 feet wide by 20 feet wide were also constructed by the government in Dundas Town to assist residents. Similar size houses were built in Murphy Town but constructed out of brick. Several of these structures survived the devastation of Hurricane Dorian.

Photos of houses that were built by the government to house persons relocated to Murphy and Dundas Town after a devastating hurricane.

A JOYFUL REUNION

CHAPTER ELEVEN

FINDING ASSISTANCE

Upon arrival in New Providence we were informed by friends and family members of various agencies that were established to assist hurricane victims. We decided to take advantage of these opportunities beginning the following day. Our first agency set up near the airport in the western district was well organized. We were greeted warmly and offered water, sandwiches and various types of snacks. I was much impressed with the level of professionalism as they inquired about our experience and empathized with us. They requested pertinent information such as name, age, address, and telephone contact. They then directed us to nearby tents where toiletries, clothing, food and other essential items were available.

At a second agency we met extremely long lines and had to wait for at least two hours before we could be interviewed. This one was not so well organized. It was clear that the workers were not prepared and understandably so. This situation was unexpected and it was difficult to properly accommodate the huge number of persons seeking assistance.

TRIUMPH IN THE MIDST OF TRAGEDY

One worker after calling three to four names to enter the interview room would shout, 'You all move it, move it." In my mind I wondered if she had any clue of what we had experienced just a few hours earlier. How could one be so insensitive and void of compassion in a case of human suffering especially when employed in the capacity as a social service worker? Perhaps she too was frustrated with this new setting of overcrowding and increased amount of work. However, the day was saved by a very pleasant lady who came and offered assistance to the many senior citizens who were sitting or standing around. Though obviously overwhelmed by the huge crowd, she maintained a pleasant and helpful disposition getting the elderly in and out of interviews as quickly as possible. I was most impressed and I wish to commend her and others like her who demonstrate care and concern in the midst of a most difficult situation.

Finally, I arrived at the front of the line and provided the requested information. All of the seats were taken and so I stood near the wall awaiting a vacant seat. After about fifteen minutes, a family became impatient and decided to leave. I quickly occupied one of the vacant seats and began conversation with several persons familiar to me. All around people were complaining of fatigue and frustration with the long wait but they were prepared to stay because they needed help.

Numerous horror stories from the hurricane were being rehearsed. Many still did not know what to make of this event. Finally, my name was called for the interview. It was quick only requiring a few answers to questions concerning my immediate needs and the presentation of identification. I was then told to return to the front and wait for a food voucher. Back at the front I inquired as to whether or not I could return the following day to collect the voucher and was told that I could.

The following day we moved to another agency set up to

assist—the agency we considered to be the main agency for disasters. Family members were told, "we are not providing assistance to persons who are living in private homes only to those in shelters." This was most disappointing and heart breaking. It was not so much what was said, but the harsh way in which it was presented. Again, I wondered if the seriousness of the situation was understood by workers at this key agency. I am aware that it all happened quickly, but if there was one agency that should have been prepared and that should have understood our mental and physical needs it should have been this particular one.

Later that day, we made our appearance at another organization providing assistance. Again, we met an overwhelmingly huge crowd and long lines. Persons did their best to accommodate us although it took hours to get in for interviews. A food voucher, water, clothing, bed linen and toiletries were provided. Grateful for the assistance, I returned home with a resolve to never stand on such long lines again.

CHAPTER TWELVE

TRAGEDY AND TRIUMPH

As I traveled through New Providence, I encountered numerous persons from Abaco and some from Grand Bahama who had weathered the storm. Stories of struggle, survival and near death experiences caused goosebumps over my body and brought me to tears. Comments such as, "Only God's mercy saved us", or "If it wasn't for God, I would have been dead" were heard continuously throughout the conversations.

One lady stated that the water came up so high in the motel that she was in that she had to climb to the rafters with her daughter and grandson to avoid drowning. The water continued to rise causing them to attempt to knock a hole in the roof, but to no avail. As if by divine inspiration the thought came to tie her daughter and grandson to her body using a jacket. Suddenly the fierce winds blew off a piece of the roof creating an opening and before she could think, they were swept through the hole in the roof into the deep water. For what seemed like hours, they were tossed to and fro by strong winds holding on to poles and trees until eventually they were rescued during the eye of the hurricane.

TRIUMPH IN THE MIDST OF TRAGEDY

A gentleman recounted how when he was blown out of his house into the water he began to pray and suddenly he saw a chest freezer floating toward him. He grabbed on to it until it landed him near a building that had not fallen. He was able to jump off and take refuge in the building.

A family friend out of Murphy Town told me that she decided to ride the storm out in her home with her son and two young grandchildren. The winds were so horrific that the grandchildren began to panic. She tried to console them, but shortly after, her son looked out the window and exclaimed that the neighbor's roof was gone. Within minutes they heard a loud cracking sound only to realize that one section of her roof was gone. Her son quickly pulled everyone into the closet and left to look for help, returning with a male family friend. The son and friend assisted her and the children to another neighbor's house that still seemed to be in good condition. Unfortunately, soon after their arrival, that roof blew away and they and the neighbors had to run in search of shelter. Someone in a van pulled up and took them in and drove them to another house. The fierce winds made it impossible for them to get out of the vehicle for a while as the vehicle was being tossed vehemently from side to side. At this point she continued to pray as it appeared they would die. After sometime the vehicle steadied enough for them to jump out and run to safety. The house they entered had minimal roof damage, but water was up to their knees. Nevertheless, they stayed the night and were rescued the following day by search and rescued teams.

Several other persons shared their experiences of being stuck in ceilings for hours praying for help. One individual shared of a close encounter with a shark when a massive sea surge destroyed their home leaving them to swim for their lives. Yet others who had never swum before stated how they had to swim to safety when their house was compromised. Some clung to tree branches for days while others witnessed their children, husbands, wives and neighbors swept away. Many were left desperately searching for loved ones who went missing in the storm, with several bodies found and dozens unaccounted for.

As the stories unfolded over the days, weeks and months, it was clear that numerous lives had been lost and hundreds were missing. Today, there has been no accurate account of the number of persons who died during the hurricane, particularly for the shanty town communities.

Survivors were overwhelmed with grief, concerns and fear. What would the future hold for us? Many were now relocating to New Providence, the country's capital city. The quiet peaceful life in tranquil settlements where everyone knew everyone was suddenly changed by Dorian. Most schools were badly damaged or destroyed and so persons had to leave even if they did not want to. The education of their children was priority. Additionally, most of the churches in the central area of Abaco had been destroyed. Pastors and their congregations were scattered. Homes and businesses were gone.

Despite this overwhelming tragedy and setback, there was a resolve among many to return and rebuild as soon as possible.

CHAPTER THIRTEEN

OUR GRATITUDE

In the wake of the hurricane there was an outpouring of concern and offers of generous support from individuals, charities, organizations and countries around the world. Among them was the US Agency for International Development and Britain's Royal Fleet Auxiliary who immediately began the delivery of food and water.

Search-and-rescue teams combed, desperately, hoping to find survivors and bodies. By Thursday, September 4th, the US Coast Guard reported they had rescued 201 residents.

Huge shipments of canned goods, water, cleaning supplies, toiletries, clothing, generators, and other urgently needed items were shipped in by many groups. Millions of dollars in pledges were made to assist in the rebuilding of the nation.

Among the most visible and memorable organizations were Samaritan Purse and World Central Kitchen. Samaritan Purse, an organization headed by Franklin Graham, brought in a well-staffed and equipped portable hospital to assist Grand Bahamians with urgent medical care. Assistance was also provided at medical facilities in Abaco.

World Central Kitchen positioned itself near the dock in

TRIUMPH IN THE MIDST OF TRAGEDY

Marsh Harbour providing hundreds of sandwiches daily. Daily nutritious hot meals were also being prepared and sent to every settlement on the island. Additionally, this organization brought much relief to our communities by providing fruits and vegetables to the various settlements on a weekly basis.

Many of our Caribbean neighbors arrived to show support and assist with cleanup and rebuilding.

In the aftermath of Dorian, several organizations saw to the repairs of roofs and renovation of the interior of houses.

This outpouring of love and acts of kindness will forever be held dear to our hearts. Gratitude and heartfelt thanks is extended to those who so graciously assisted us and for this we are extremely grateful.

CHAPTER FOURTEEN

LESSONS FROM DORIAN

Hurricane Dorian has imparted many lessons. Paramount among them is the importance of hurricane preparedness. Hurricanes should always be taken seriously and adequate preparations made to minimize the loss of life. Proper hurricane shelters should be erected and persons in low lying areas or homes that may easily be compromised should move immediately when instructions are given to do so.

Perhaps more attention should be paid to global warming as it seems to now be posing serious threats to our global community. According to climate experts the Earth is warming up at a steady pace due to the increase in human-caused greenhouse gases, which has led to health, ecological and humanitarian crises. The increase in temperature has led to sea level rise and it has been forecasted that tropical storms will be even stronger due to sea water temperature rising. It is also anticipated that the frequency and strength of these storms or phenomena will be enhanced or increased due to rising sea temperatures.

Temperature is also impacting the marine environment in terms of coral bleaching which leads to acidification and death due to the release of methane gas in marine environments which also assist in the temperature rise because it impacts the ozone.

Rise in sea temperature has also led to northward migration of stock normally associated with the South Caribbean. Additionally, uncommon marine diseases are affecting reefs in The Bahamas. The Stony Coral virus was discovered in Grand Bahama and is now being found in the area of New Providence.

The increasing strength of storms leads to higher tidal surges. During Dorian, tidal surges especially in the Abaco area were over 20 feet above normal.

These tidal surges during Hurricane Dorian resulted in the influx of salt into the soil negatively affecting the health of the plants. In addition to salt water damage, the heavy winds destroyed lots of crops and animals.

Dorian also affected the fishing sector causing destruction to the reefs and turbidity of the sea bed impacting oxygen levels and clarity. A report uploaded by the Weather Channel, February, 2020 stated that in addition to causing devastation on land the hurricane also destroyed roughly 30% of the coral reef around The Bahamas. Reefs are a major part of our economy since they are among our major tourist attractions. In addition, the impact of this hurricane also resulted in the loss of fishing gear (traps) and fishing vessels preventing fishermen from making a living.

It is believed that climate change impacts rising sea levels and research has shown that climate change also impacts the amount of water in the atmosphere and will increasingly produce violent downpours when it rains. This suggests that hurricanes will increase in power, and flooding will become more common. With this in mind, more should be done in our country to educate the population on global warming and its effects. Further, effort must be ongoing to educate individuals on the value of protecting our reefs.

Already our country is considering improving our building code. Though this code is high compared to many countries,

Dorian has made us aware that it has to be strengthened if we are to withstand future category five hurricanes with wind speed of 185 miles per hour or more.

Additionally, from the massive destruction of buildings on the waterfront, we may now have to consider building further in land and where possible in more elevated areas. This may minimize the effects of sea surges on buildings.

Life is uncertain and as such we must strive to build our faith in God. Our country has been established as a Christian nation. As such, our faith in Him must be unwavering. We are admonished in Proverbs 3:5-6, to:

Trust in the Lord with all thine heart; And lean not unto thine own understanding. In all thy ways kacknowledge him, And lhe shall direct thy paths.

Psalm 125:1 says:
They that trust in the Lord shall be as mount Zion, which cannot be removed, but abideth for ever.

As a people let us resolve to trust Him. Finally, let us seek to be our brothers' keepers, love each other sincerely as commanded in scripture, develop a bonding with family- and maintain meaningful relationships with each other.

The hurricane should serve to make us better, not bitter. From my experience in Dorian I emerged:

- with a heart of gratitude
- thankful to be alive
- with the desire to never again take life or people for granted.

I am eternally grateful to God for protecting us during what I would refer to as a cataclysmic event.

ABOUT THE AUTHOR
Ms. E. McIntosh

Ethlene McIntosh was born and raised on the island of Abaco, Bahamas. She is a veteran educator whose career spans more than thirty years of providing classroom instruction in both primary and secondary school education and also as a school administrator with the Department of Education in The Bahamas.

Ethlene earned her Master's Degree in Business Administration from Nova Southeastern University in Fort Lauderdale, Florida., a Bachelor of Arts Degree from University of the West Indies, Mona, Jamaica and a Teachers Certificate from the College of The Bahamas (now University of The Bahamas); She has also attended numerous conferences, workshops, and training sessions locally and internationally.

Her true passion is for helping others to be inspired, motivated, educated, and to work hard in order to achieve their goals. Additionally, she has spent many years assisting the youth of her nation in identifying their purpose and helping them to become productive citizens of their country. She is also an avid historian and social observer, who is always on the look-out for ways to increase the level of social awareness and national pride of those around her.

Ethlene is a woman of compassion and prayer and is presently actively involved in church ministry, serving as an Elder with responsibility for prayer and intercession at her church, Lifegate Christian Ministries International in Abaco.

In 2007, she was honored by Women of Influence for her outstanding contribution and dedicated service to Christian Ministry and Education.

A very versatile lady, Ethlene enjoys the outdoors and the beauty of nature. She loves gardening, reading, travelling and encouraging others.

www.ingramcontent.com/pod-product-compliance
Lightning Source LLC
Chambersburg PA
CBHW052124110526
44592CB00013B/1743